THE BEATLES FOR TWO

Arrangements by Mark Phillips

Cover photo: CBS Photo Archive via Getty Images

ISBN 978-1-5400-4813-4

Visit Hal Leonard Online at
www.halleonard.com

Contact us:
Hal Leonard
7777 West Bluemound Road
Milwaukee, WI 53213
Email: info@halleonard.com

In Europe, contact:
Hal Leonard Europe Limited
42 Wigmore Street
Marylebone, London, W1U 2RN
Email: info@halleonardeurope.com

In Australia, contact:
Hal Leonard Australia Pty. Ltd.
4 Lentara Court
Cheltenham, Victoria, 3192 Australia
Email: info@halleonard.com.au

ALL MY LOVING

FLUTES

Words and Music by JOHN LENNON
and PAUL McCARTNEY

ALL YOU NEED IS LOVE

FLUTES

Words and Music by JOHN LENNON
and PAUL McCARTNEY

AND I LOVE HER

FLUTES

Words and Music by JOHN LENNON
and PAUL McCARTNEY

ELEANOR RIGBY

FLUTES

Words and Music by JOHN LENNON
and PAUL McCARTNEY

THE FOOL ON THE HILL

FLUTES

Words and Music by JOHN LENNON
and PAUL McCARTNEY

Moderately slow, in 2

GOLDEN SLUMBERS

FLUTES

Words and Music by JOHN LENNON
and PAUL McCARTNEY

HERE COMES THE SUN

FLUTES

Words and Music by
GEORGE HARRISON

Moderately fast

HERE, THERE AND EVERYWHERE

FLUTES

Words and Music by JOHN LENNON
and PAUL McCARTNEY

HEY JUDE

FLUTES

Words and Music by JOHN LENNON
and PAUL McCARTNEY

I SAW HER STANDING THERE

FLUTES

Words and Music by JOHN LENNON
and PAUL McCARTNEY

I WANT TO HOLD YOUR HAND

Flutes

Words and Music by JOHN LENNON
and PAUL McCARTNEY

Moderately fast

I WILL

FLUTES

Words and Music by JOHN LENNON
and PAUL McCARTNEY

Moderately

LET IT BE

FLUTES

Words and Music by JOHN LENNON
and PAUL McCARTNEY

THE LONG AND WINDING ROAD

FLUTES

Words and Music by JOHN LENNON
and PAUL McCARTNEY

MICHELLE

FLUTES

Words and Music by JOHN LENNON
and PAUL McCARTNEY

NORWEGIAN WOOD
(This Bird Has Flown)

FLUTES

Words and Music by JOHN LENNON
and PAUL McCARTNEY

OB-LA-DI, OB-LA-DA

FLUTES

Words and Music by JOHN LENNON
and PAUL McCARTNEY

PENNY LANE

FLUTES

Words and Music by JOHN LENNON
and PAUL McCARTNEY

SHE LOVES YOU

FLUTES

Words and Music by JOHN LENNON
and PAUL McCARTNEY

Moderately fast

SOMETHING

FLUTES

Words and Music by
GEORGE HARRISON

WHEN I'M SIXTY-FOUR

FLUTES

Words and Music by JOHN LENNON
and PAUL McCARTNEY

YELLOW SUBMARINE

FLUTES

Words and Music by JOHN LENNON
and PAUL McCARTNEY

YESTERDAY

FLUTES

Words and Music by JOHN LENNON
and PAUL McCARTNEY